Illustrated Catalogue And Price List Of Copper Weather Vanes, Bannerets And Finials / Manufactured By A.b. & W.t. Westervelt.

A.B. & W.T. Westervelt (New York, N.Y.)

No. 6.

Illustrated Catalogue

AND

PRICE LIST

OF

COPPER WEATHER VANES, BANNERETS

AND FINIALS,

MANUFACTURED BY

A. B. & W. T. WESTERVELT,

OFFICE AND WAREROOMS:

1   ^^AMBERS STREET,

h St   NEW YORK.

CUPOLA AND VANE.

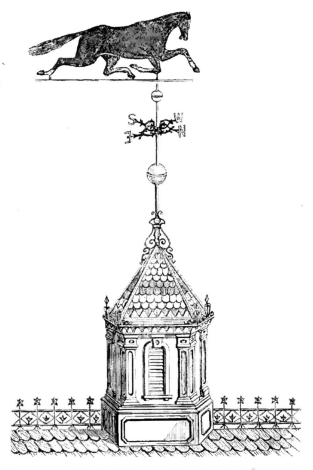

This cut represents a Cupola and Vane, mounted complete, showing the proper position of Balls and Points of Compass. If no compass is at hand to set the cardinal points by, notice that the sun is exactly in the South at meridian (or noon).

DIRECTIONS FOR PUTTING UP VANE

Bore or cut a hole perfectly perpendicular—care must be taken i.   is a   hole
will make the Vane stand crooked—the hole should be a little larger th   ize   ire,
wedge in tight and straight. Fill any crevices or joints with White Lead
should be set in from 8 to 12 inches, and for a very large Vane, 18 inches to

NOTE.—Avoid handling the gilding with the bare hands; han
tissue-paper, cotton or soft cloth.

All the tools necessary are a screw driver, with which to fasten the
Ring for lower Ball to Spire, and brace and bit or chisel, to make the hole f
                                                                        r.

PREFACE.

In compiling this (the sixth) edition of our Illustrated Catalogue of Weather Vanes, Bannerets and Finials, we have endeavored to include appropriate designs for Churches, Public Buildings, Residences, Stables, Barns, &c., &c., thus making it the most complete work issued; we are, however, continually adding new and original designs to our stock.

Our Vanes are made **Entirely of Copper** *and* **Gilded with the Finest Gold Leaf,** *will keep bright, will not corrode, and are perfect indicators of the wind's direction.*

The letters and balls are well gilded, the spires are of wrought iron, with hardened steel spindles for the Vanes to turn upon.

Our Copper Eagles, *from the largest to the smallest, for* **Vanes** *or* **Architectural** *purposes, are full-bodied, the wings of double thickness, and are a perfect representation of the* **American Eagle.**

The Price of each Vane includes a Wrought Iron Spire with points of Compass, Gilt Letters and Balls.

Vanes of any design or size, to order on short notice and at reasonable rates.

We would caution our customers and the public against being deceived by Vanes which are now being made, (copied after our original designs,) which are manufactured of **Sheet Zinc** *and* **covered with a thin solution of Copper with Zinc Tubing,** *unlike our Vanes, which are made of Sheet Copper and Brass Tubing.*

Special attention given to the erection of Lightning Rods, in connection with our Vanes, Crestings, Finials and Terminals. All the varieties of Galvanized Iron, Copper covered and Solid Copper Rods with Fixtures, furnished on short notice. (see page 99.)

With the view of simplifying the ordering of our Vanes, please describe each design by the name, &c., given in this book; always specifying the **Figure Number,** *size of Vane, and number of this catalogue (No. 6); also, be careful to give full and particular shipping directions.*

Experienced persons will be sent to receive instructions, to give practical information and take orders.

It will be our endeavor to ship all goods with promptness, and careful attention is given to packing.

We make our grateful acknowledgments to our customers and friends for past favors, and trust to merit their future patronage.

Respectfully

A B. & W. T. WESTERVELT.

ST. JULIAN.

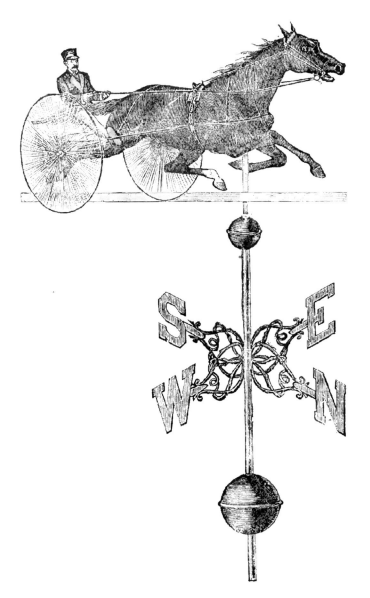

No. 301.   New design, 39 inches long, full bodied $44 00

" 302.   "   "   46   "   "   with Sulky and Driver................... 62 00

" 303.   "   "   32   "   "   swell bodied........... .... 26 00

☞ All our Vanes are made of copper, and gilded with finest gold leaf.

MAUD S.

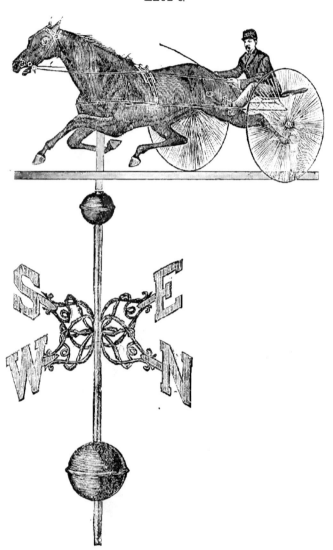

No. 304.   New design, 36 inches long, full bodied $42 00

  " 305.   "   "   44   "   "   with Sulky and Driver 60 00

  " 306.   "   "   31   "   "   swell bodied........ .... 25 00

☞ All four Vanes are made of copper, and gilded with finest gold leaf.

LARGE 48-INCH ETHAN ALLEN.

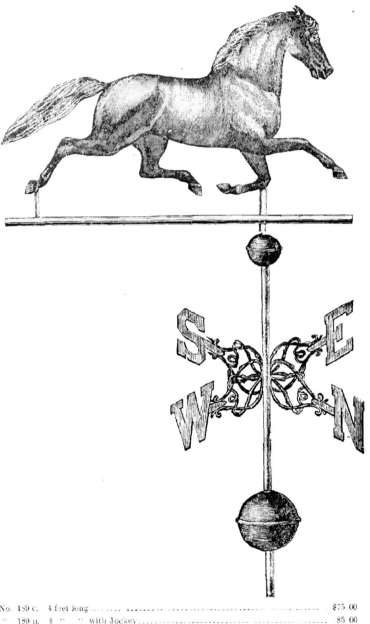

No. 189 C.   4 feet long... $75 00
"   189 D.   4 "   " with Jockey.. 85 00
"   189 E.   5 "   " " Sulky and Driver... 100 00
"   189 F.   5 " 6 inches, with Wagon and Driver.............................. 125 00

☞ All our Vanes are made of copper, and gilded with finest gold leaf.

GEORGE M. PATCHEN.

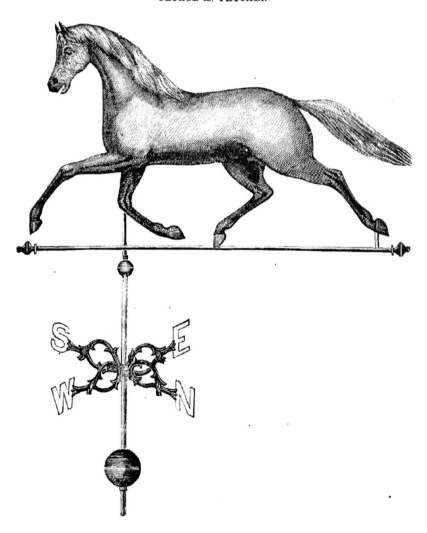

No. 186. 3 feet 6 inches long, swell bodied...$40 00

" 187. 4 " 4 " " with Sulky and Driver................................... 60 00

" 187½. 5 " long, with Wagon " " 65 00

☞The price of each Vane includes an iron spire, appropriate letters and balls complete.

BLACK HAWK.

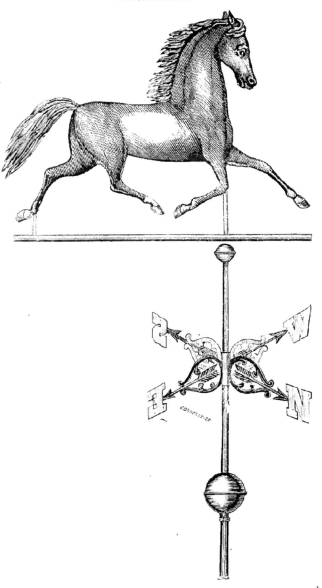

No. 181.	26 inches long....		.......$17 00
" 182.	36 "	" with Sulky and Driver.	27 00
" 182½.	33 "	"	35 00
" 182A.	40 "	" with Sulky and Driver	45 00
" 182B.	44 "	" " Wagon "	50 00

☞ All our Vanes are made of copper, and gilded with finest gold leaf.

NEW DESIGN.—STALLION.

No. 163. 28 inches long, full bodied..$50 00

☞All our Vanes are made of copper, and gilded with finest gold leaf.

ETHAN ALLEN.

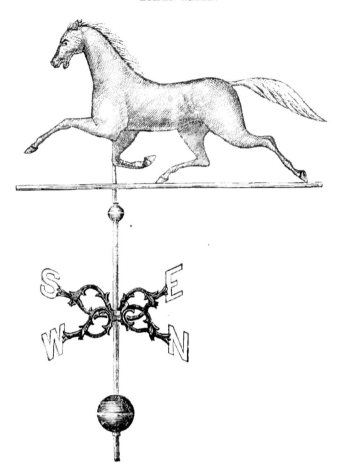

Large, Handsome, Showy Horse Vane, at a Low Price.

SWELL BODIED, COPPER.

No, 189.	31 inches long				$20 00
" 189½.	36 "	"	with Sulky and Driver		30 00
" 189A.	31 "	"	"	Jockey	25 00
" 189B.	39 "	"	"	Wagon and Driver	35 00

☞ All complete as above, with Spire, Letters and Balls.

Note.—Our Vanes are gilded with finest gold leaf, and on copper, warranted to stand the weather in any climate, and not tarnish or corrode.

HAMBLETONIAN.

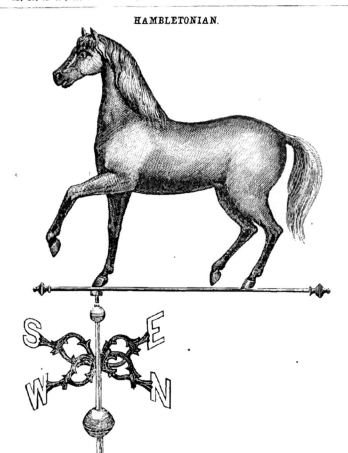

No. 166.   New design, 26 inches long $25 00

ARABIAN.

No. 304A.   17 inches long, mounted complete as shown above $14 00

DEXTER.

No. 167. 43 inches long.. $40 00

"   172. 43   "   " with Jockey.. 50 00

"   170. 52   "   "   " Sulky and Driver..................................... 55 00

"   173. 57   "   "   " Wagon and Driver.................................... 75 00

"   174. 34   "   " 22 00

"   174½. 34   "   " with Jockey.. 27 00

'   175. 42   "   "   " Sulky and Driver..................................... 32 00

"   176. 50   "   "   " Wagon and Driver.................................... 40 00

☞ All our Vanes are made of copper, and gilded with finest gold leaf.

DEXTER.

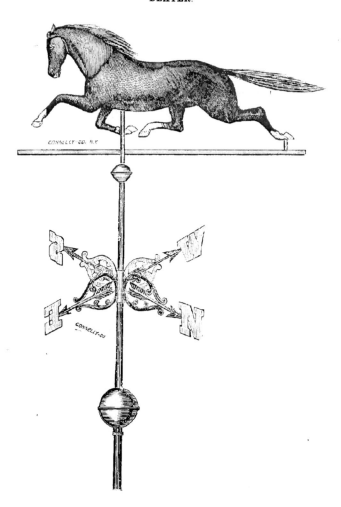

No. 168 A3.   26 inches long, new design, full bodied.............................$25 00
"   168½A3.   26   "   with Jockey.. 30 00
"   169 A3.   34   "   "   Sulky and Driver........................... 35 00
"   165 B3.   42   "   new design, full bodied.......................... 50 00
"   165½B3.   42   "   with Jockey.. 65 00
"   171 B3.   58   "   "   Sulky and Driver........................... 75 00

☞ All our Vanes are made of copper, and gilded with finest gold leaf.

DEXTER, WITH JOCKEY.

No. 176½. 42 inches long, full bodied, with Jockey........ ... . $65 00

"   177.   43   "   "   swell   "   "   " 50 00

"   178.   34   "   "   "   "   "   " 27 00

"   178½. 26   "   "   full   "   "   " 30 00

☞ All our Vanes are made of copper, and gilded with finest gold leaf.

FOXHALL, WITH JOCKEY.—New Design.

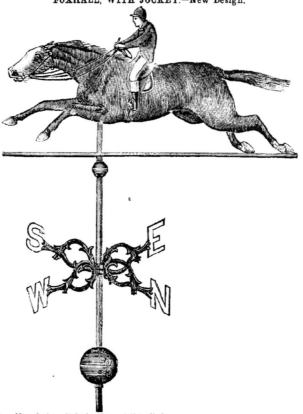

No. 305A. New design, 31 inches long, full bodied $30 00
" 308A. " " 31 " " without Jockey 25 00

KENTUCKY, WITH JOCKEY.

No. 179. New design, 32 inches long, full bodied, mounted complete, as shown above . $30 00
" 180. " without Jockey, mounted complete, as shown above 25 00

☞ All our Vanes are made of copper, and gilded with finest gold leaf.

GOLDSMITH MAID.

NEW DESIGN, FULL BODIED.

No. 183.	32 inches long		$30 00
" 184.	40 "	with Sulky and Driver	45 00
" 185.	46 "	" Wagon "	50 00

LEXINGTON.

No. 188 35 inches long, mounted complete, as shown above............ ....$30 00

SMUGGLER.

A VERY ATTRACTIVE VANE, FULL OF ACTION.

No. 164. 31 inches long $20 00
" 164A. 31   "   with Jockey 25 00
" 164B. 36   "   " Sulky and Driver 30 00

FARM HORSE.

No. 164½. 18 inches long, mounted complete, as shown above $14 00

☞All our Vanes are made of copper, and gilded with finest gold leaf.

HORSE TO WAGON.

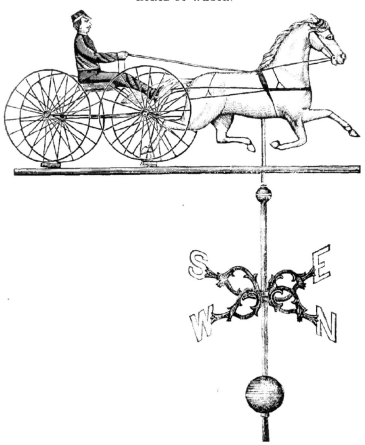

No. 194½   Horse to Wagon, 46 inches long. $50 00

MOUNTAIN BOY

No. 194½   33 inches long, new design, full bodied, mounted complete, as shown above.$35 00

☞ All our Vanes are made of copper, and gilded with finest gold leaf.

ETHAN ALLEN, Jr.

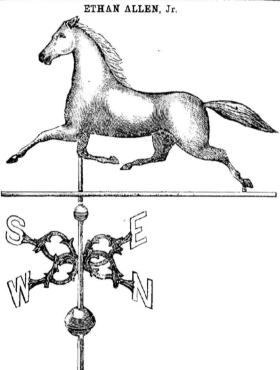

No. 190.   26 inches long..$15 00
"   190A. 30   "   with Sulky and Driver......................... 25 00
"   190B.26   "   "   Jockey.. 30 00

AMERICAN GIRL.

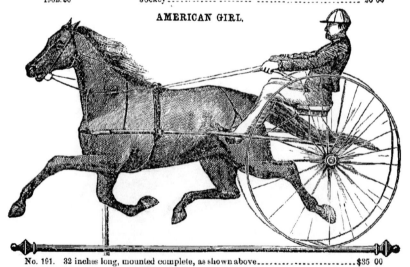

No. 191.   32 inches long, mounted complete, as shown above....................$35 00
"   192.   36   "   with Sulky and Driver, mounted complete, as shown above. 45 00
"   193.   42   "   "   Wagon and Driver   "   "   "   "   50 00

SHORT HORNED JERSEY COW.

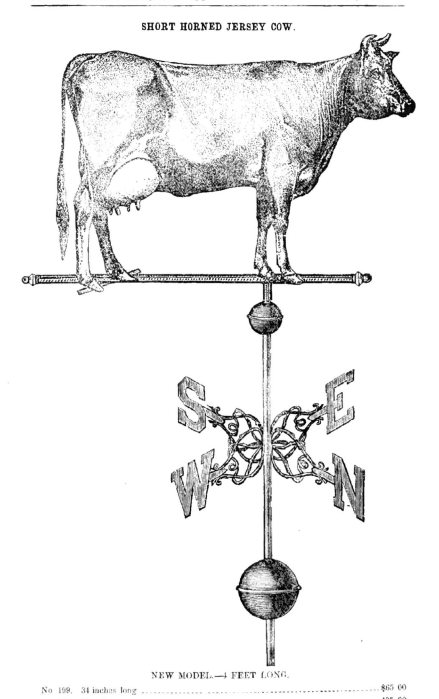

NEW MODEL.—4 FEET LONG.

No 199. 34 inches long $65 00
" 200. 48 "   " 125 00

BULL.

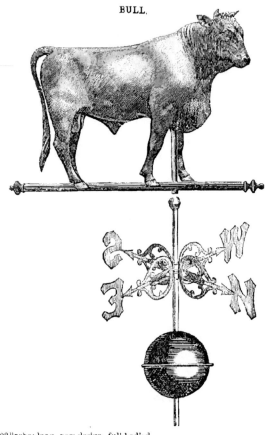

No. 195. 28 inches long, new design, full bodied $50 00
" 195½. 36 "   "   "   " 125 00
" 195A. 48 "   "   "   " 175 00

COW.

No. 196. 28 inches long, full bodied, mounted complete as shown above............$30 00
" 197. 42 " " old design, "   " 77 00
" 198. 24 " " 20 00

OX.

No. 201.	Old design, 28 inches long, mounted complete, as shown below									$25 00
" 202.	"	24	"	"	"	"	"	"		20 00
" 203.	New design 42	"	"	"	"	"	"	"		75 00
" 204.	"	34	"	"	"	"	"	"		65 00
" 204½.	"	36	"	"	"	"	"	"		100 00
" 204A.	"	48	"	"	"	"	"	"		125 00

HOG.

No. 207.	3 feet long	$35 00
" 208.	3 " 6 inches long	50 00
" 208½.	4 " long	60 00

☞ All our Vanes are made of copper, and gilded with finest gold leaf.

MERINO RAM, ETHAN ALLEN.

No. 206½.   3 feet long, mounted complete, as shown below........................$50 00

SHEEP.

No. 205.   28 inches long..$25 00

Any other style or size to order.

MERINO RAM, SWEEPSTAKES.

No. 206.   2 feet 6 inches long, mounted complete, as shown above.................$32 00
"   206A. 3 feet long,   "   "   "   " 50 00

SPORTSMAN'S DOG.

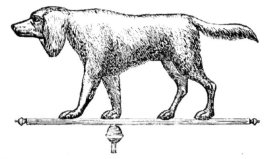

No. 71. 33 inches long, swell bodied, mounted complete, as shown opposite........$25 00

DOLPHIN OR DRAGON VANE.

No. 72. 26 inches long, full bodied, mounted complete, as shown opposite..........$35 00

OSCEOLA CHIEF.

No. 72½. 30 inches high, mounted complete, as shown opposite.....................$40 00

☞Other sizes and styles to order.

LION.

No. 65. 3 feet long, mounted complete, as shown below.........................$80 00
" 66. 4 " " " 125 00

LION AND VANE.

No. 67. 12x24 inches, swell bodied lion, arrow, 3 feet 6 inches long..............$40 00

RUNNING DEER.

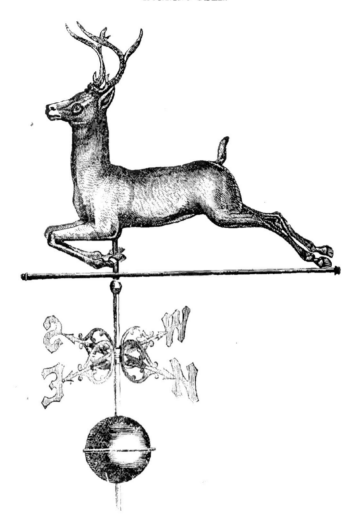

No. 231. New design, 50 inches long, full bodied........ ....$90 00

" 232.   "   36   "   " 50 00

" 233.   "   20   "   " 30 00

" 234.   "   30   "   " 40 00

☞ All our Vanes are made of copper, and gilded with finest gold leaf.

AMERICAN MOOSE DEER.

No. 235.	2 feet long, full bodied		$30 00
" 235½.	2 feet 6 inches long, full bodied		40 00
" 235A.	3 " " "		50 00

Other sizes to order.

LEAPING DEER.—New Design.

No. 236.	31 inches long, mounted complete, as shown above		$40 00
" 236½.	31 " without bush, " "		35 00

FISH VANE.—New Design.

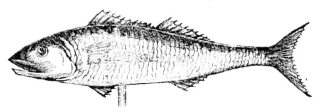

No. 307.   30 inches long, new design, full bodied, mounted complete, as shown below, $30 00

"   308.   38   "   "   "   "   "   "   "   "   40 00

FISH VANE.

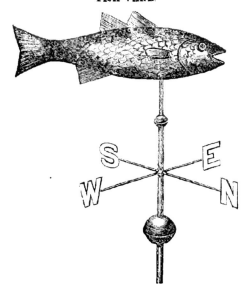

No. 209½.   18 inches long, full bodied..$15 50

"   209.   24   "   " 17 50

"   210.   30   "   " 20 00

"   210½.   36   "   " 30 00

"   210A.   42   "   " 40 00

FISH SIGNS.—Flat.

No. 211.   Fish for swinging signs, 9 inches long........ ....$3 00

"   212.   "   "   " 16   " 4 00

Any size of the above styles to order.

☞ The price of each Vane includes a wrought iron spire, points of compass, and gilt letters and balls.

NEW DESIGN, PIGEON ON BALL, WITH ARROW.

(WINGS SPREAD.)

No. 146.   New design, full bodied, 18 inches high, including ball and arrow, with 2 feet arrow......$28 00
" 117.   "   "   18   "   "   "   "   "   2 ft. 6 in. arrow...32 00

NEW DESIGN, PIGEON ON BALL, WITH ARROW.

(WINGS FOLDED.)

No. 148.   New design, full bodied, 18 inches high, including ball and arrow, with 2 feet arrow ... $20 00
" 149.   "   "   18   "   "   "   "   "   2 " 6 in. arrow   24 00
Mounted complete, as shown above.

☞ All our Vanes are made of copper, and gilded with finest gold leaf.

NEW DESIGN, CROWING ROOSTER ON BALL, WITH ARROW. (Wings Spread.)

No. 142. New design, full bodied rooster, 21 inches high (including ball and arrow), with 2 feet 6 inches arrow..$38 00
" 143. With 2 feet arrow.. 35 00

NEW DESIGN, CROWING ROOSTER ON BALL, WITH ARROW. (Wings Closed.)

No. 144. New design, full bodied crowing rooster, 21 inches high (including ball and arrow), with 2 feet 6 inches arrow,......................................$34 00
" 145. With 2 feet arrow.. 30 00

GAME ROOSTER.

No 102. 18 inches high, double thickness copper...$10 00

GAME ROOSTER AND ARROW VANE.

No. 153. 18 inches high, with 24 inch arrow, double thickness copper..............$15 00
" 154. 18   "   "   30   "   "   "   "   20 00

CROWING ROOSTER.

No. 155. 36 inches high...$40 00

"   156. 24   " 30 00

"   157. 18   " 20 00

EAGLE AND ARROW.—New Design.

No. 77. 6 inch spread eagle and 24 inch arrow, mounted complete, as shown above...$12 00

"   78. 6 "   "   "   30 "   "   "   "   "   .. 15 00

"   79. 12 "   "   "   36 "   "   "   "   "   .. 20 00

"   79½.15 "   "   "   42 "   "   "   "   "   .. 30 00

☞All our Vanes are made of copper, and gilded with finest gold leaf.

MEDIÆVAL ROOSTER VANE FOR CHURCHES.

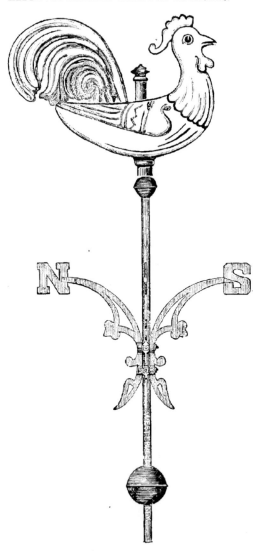

No. 309. 2 feet 6 inches high, as shown above..$50 00

"   310. 3 "   "   "   " 70 00

"   311. 2 " 6 inches "   mounted as shown on page 34....... .... 40 00

"   312. 3 "   "   "   "   " 60 00

☞All our Vanes are made of copper, and gilded with finest gold leaf.

NEW DESIGN ROOSTER AND ARROW VANE.

No. 150.   15 inches high, with 18 inch Arrow..$14 00
"   151.   26   "   "   30   " 30 00
"   152.   32   "   "   36   " 40 00
"   152½. 42   "   "   60   " 60 00

☞ All our Vanes are made of copper, and gilded with finest gold leaf.

NEW DESIGN ROOSTER VANE.

Engraved from a photograph of our Work.

(SWELL BODIED, COPPER.)

No. 158.	36 inches high	....	\$35 00	with 4 feet arrow	....	\$50 00
" 159.	28 "	....	25 00	" 3 " "	....	40 00
" 160.	24 "	....	15 00	" 30 inches "	....	25 00
" 161.	14 "	....	7 50	" 24 " "	....	15 00

Rooster standing on Arrow, as shown on page 31—Game Rooster.

EAGLE AND PEN VANE.

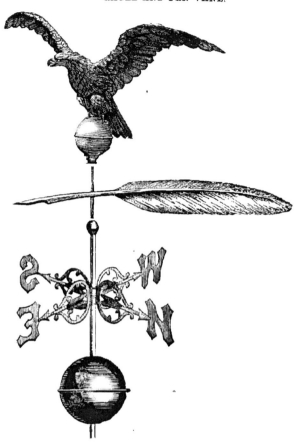

Very handsome, attractive Vanes, especially designed for Schools, Colleges, Academies, Newspaper Buildings, &c., &c.

No. 92.	8 feet spread	with 10 feet Pen,	$275 00
" 93.	7 " "	" 8 "	225 00
" 94.	6 " 6 inches spread	" 7½ "	200 00
" 95.	5 " 6 "	" 6½ "	175 00
" 96.	5 " spread	" 6 "	150 00
" 97.	4 " 6 inches spread	" 5½ "	110 00
" 98.	4 " spread	" 5 "	85 00
" 99.	3 " 6 inches spread	" 4½ "	65 00
" 100.	3 " spread	" 4 "	55 00
" 101.	2 " 6 inches spread	" 3½ "	50 00
" 102.	2 " spread	" 3 "	35 00
" 103.	1 " 6 inches spread	" 30 inch Pen,	25 00
" 104.	1 " 3 "	" 24 "	18 00
" 105.	1 " spread	" 18 "	12 00

COPPER EAGLE WITH ARROW.

Engraved from a Photograph of our work.

We make a PERFECT EAGLE, wholly of Copper, with double thick wings.

Arrows are indispensable when Eagles are used as Vanes.

No. 106.	12 feet spread	$500 00
" 107.	10 " "	425 00
" 108.	8 " "	300 00
" 109.	7 " "	225 00
" 110.	6 " 6 inches spread	185 00
" 111.	5 " 6 "	150 00
" 112.	5 " spread	135 00
" 113.	4 " "	70 00
" 114.	3 " 6 inches spread	50 00
" 115.	3 " spread	47 00
" 116.	2 " 6 inches spread	35 00
" 117.	2 " spread	25 00
" 118.	1 foot 6 inches spread	21 00
" 119.	1 " 3 "	15 00
" 120.	1 " spread	10 00

NEW DESIGN EAGLE AND SCROLL VANE.

No. 121. Eagle, 15 inches spread with 3 feet scroll............................ $28 00
" 122. " 20 " " 3½ " 35 00
" 123. " 30 " " 4 " 45 00
" 124. " 36 " " 5 " 75 00
" 124½. " 48 " " 6 " 100 00

☞ All our Vanes are made of copper, and gilded with finest gold leaf.

EAGLES WITHOUT ARROWS FOR FLAG POLES.—Of Copper.

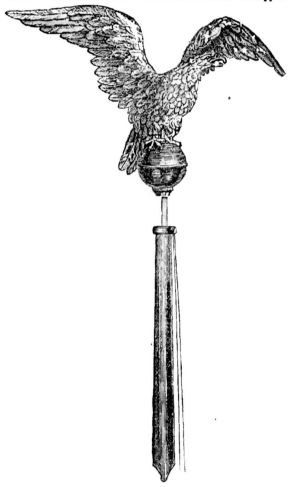

No. 125.	6 inches spread, on ball and base or ball and stem	$4 00
" 126.	12 " " " " "	9 00
" 127.	15 " " " " " "	12 00
" 128.	18 " " " " " "	15 00
" 129.	24 " " " " " "	20 00
" 130.	30 " " " " " "	31 00
" 131.	36 " " " " " "	37 00
" 132.	42 " " " " " "	40 00
" 133.	48 " " " " " "	60 00
" 134.	4 feet 6 inches spread, on ball and base or ball and stem	70 00
" 135.	5 " " " " " "	110 00
" 136.	5 " 6 " " " " "	125 00
" 137.	6 " " " " " "	140 00
" 138.	6 " 6 " " " " "	150 00
" 139.	7 " " " " " "	170 00
" 140.	7 " 6 " " " " "	200 00
" 141.	8 " " " " " "	225 00

☞ All our Vanes are made of copper, and gilded with finest gold leaf.

CAST ZINC EAGLES

For Flag Poles, Lamps, Store Signs, Monuments, &c , are not suitable for Vanes

3 inches spread.		$1 25
4 "		2 25
6½ "		3 25
7 "		4 00
10 "		5 00
13 "		8 00
14 "		10 00
18 "		15 00
22 "		16 50
30 "		24 00
31 "		38 00
50 "		50 00
60 "		96 00

FLAG POLES.

25 feet long, 5 inches diameter at Butt				$10 00
30 " 6 " "				15 00
35 " 6 " "				18 00
40 " 7 " "				23 00
40 " 8 " "				27 00
45 " 8 " "				35 00
50 " 8 " "				40 00
50 " 9 " "				45 00
55 " 9 " "				55 00
60 " 9 " "				70 00
60 " 10 " "				75 00
65 " 11 " "				100 00
70 " 11 " "				110 00

BEST LIGNUM-VITÆ TRUCKS

		Fitted with brass wheels	
3 inch	$ 50		$1 00
3½ "	70	" " "	1 20
4 "	1 00	" " "	1 40
4½ "	1 20	" " "	1 60
5 "	1 30	" " "	1 80
5½ "	1 40	" " "	2 40
6 "	2 00	" " "	3 00
7 "	2 50	" " "	3 75
8 "	3 50	" " "	5 00

METAL BALLS FOR FLAG POLES.

Metal Balls on Stems, gilded with Pure Gold Leaf, for Flag-staffs.

	Each.
3 inches	$ 70
4 "	1 10
5 "	1 40
6 "	2 00
7 "	3 00
8 "	3 50
9 "	6 00
10 "	7 75
12 "	12 00

Metal Balls, not on Stems, gilded with Pure Gold, for Vanes or other purposes.

	Each.
1 inch	$ 25
2 inches	35
2½ "	45
3 "	60
4 "	95
5 "	1 25
6 "	1 55
7 "	2 60
8 "	3 00
9 "	4 50
10 "	5 00
12 "	7 50
15 "	18 75
18 "	25 00

FLAG POLE BALLS OF BEST SEASONED WHITE WOOD.

2 inches diameter, each		$ 30
2½ " "		55
3 " "		65
4 " "		1 30
5 " "		1 80
6 " "		2 50
7 " "		3 50
8 " "		4 50
9 " "		5 50
10 " "		6 75

METAL STARS.

	9 in.	12 in.	15 in.	18 in.	24 in.
5 points	$4 00	$5 50	$7 50	$10 00	$16 00
6 "	5 00	6 50	8 50	11 00	17 00
9 "	10 00	13 00	17 00	22 00	34 00
10 "	12 00	15 00	19 00	25 00	37 00
12 "	14 00	17 00	21 00	28 00	40 00
14 "	16 00	18 00	25 00	33 00	50 00

Any other size made to order.

FLAG POLE ORNAMENTS.

Balls and 5 Points Stars.

3 in. ball, 4 in. star	$2 20		
4 " 5 "	3 50		
5 " 6 "	4 50		
6 " 7 "	5 50		
8 " 9 "	7 50		
10 " 12 "	13 25		
12 " 15 "	19 50		
15 " 18 "	25 00		

3 inch ball	$1 00
4 "	1 50
5 "	2 00
6 "	2 75
7 "	4 00
8 "	4 50
9 "	7 50
10 "	9 00
12 "	14 00

MALT SHOVEL VANE.

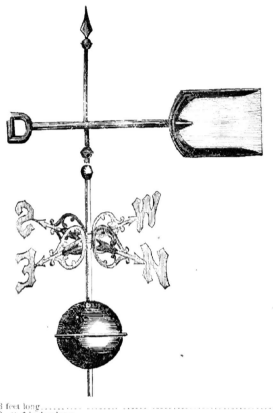

No. 51A. 3 feet long.. $25 00
  "   51½. 3 " 6 inches long.. 35 00
  "   51B. 4 " long... 50 00

HOOK AND LADDER AND NUMBER VANE.

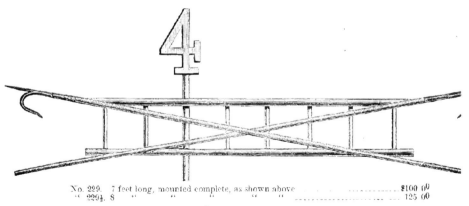

No. 229. 7 feet long, mounted complete, as shown above $100 00
  "   229½. 8   "   "   "   "   " 125 00

☞ All our Vanes are made of copper, and gilded with finest gold leaf.

HOSE CARRIAGE VANE.

No. 230. 3 feet 6 inches long, mounted complete, as shown on page 44 ....$85 00
" 230½. 4 " 6 " " " " " 44...............100 00
Also made with horse and driver. Any size made to order.

HOOK AND LADDER VANE.

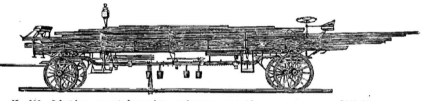

No. 226. 5 feet long, mounted complete, as shown on page 44.....................$110 00
" 226½. 6 " " " " " 44.................... 130 00
Made with horses and men to order.

STEAM FIRE ENGINE VANE.

No. 225. 7 feet long, with driver, firemen and horses........................$250 00
" 225½. 5 " " " " 175 00
Mounted complete, as shown on page 44.

☞ For Firemen's Hat and Trumpet Vane, see page 83.

LIBERTY CAP AND ARROW VANE

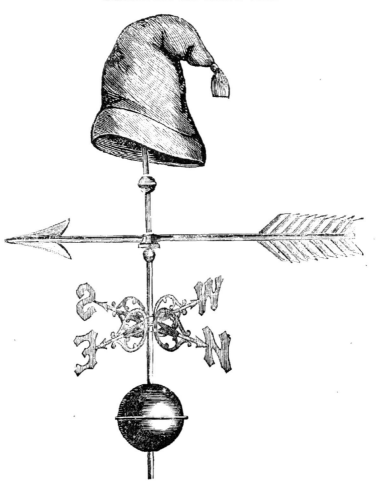

No. 25. Liberty Cap, 12 inches high, Arrow 24 inches long................................ $20 00

" 26.   "   18   "   " 30   " 40 00

" 27.   "   24   "   " 36   " 55 00

" 28.   "   36   "   " 60   ' 85 00

The price of each Vane includes a wrought iron spire with points of
compass, gilt letters and balls.

GUN AND CAP VANE.

No. 30. Gun 4 feet long, mounted complete, as shown opposite................$45 00
   "   31.   "   5   "   "   "   " 55 00
   "   32.   "   6   "   "   "   " 65 00
   "   33.   "   7   "   "   "   " 75 00
   "   34.   "   8   "   "   "   " 100 00

COPPER FLAG.

No. 42. 18 inches Flag........$12 00
   "   43.   24   " 18 00
   "   44.   36   " 30 00

LIBERTY CAP.

No. 35. 6 inches high..........$7 50
   "   36.   9   " 12 00
   "   37.   12   " 15 00
   "   38.   15   " 20 00
   "   39.   18   " 30 00
   "   40.   24   " 40 00

☞ All our Vanes are made of copper, and gilded with finest gold leaf.

GODDESS OF LIBERTY.

No. 41,   24 inches high, mounted complete, as shown below... ....$30 00
"   41A, 36   "   "   "   " 45 00
"   41B, 48   "   "   "   " 75 00

CANNON.

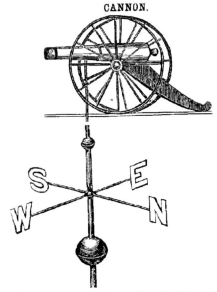

No. 45, 20 inches long............$30 00   No. 45½, 30 inches long..........$45 00

YACHT VANE.

No. 213. 3 feet long, sloop rigged, mounted complete, as shown on page 44 .... $38 00
"   214. 4   "   "   "   "   "   " 45 00
"   215. 3½ " schooner rigged,   "   "   "   " 60 00
"   216. 3   "   "   "   "   "   " 48 00

SHIP VANE.

No. 217. 3 feet long, mounted complete, as shown on page 44 .... $75 00
"   218. 4   "   "   "   "   " 100 00

Any size or design made to order.

OCEAN STEAMER.

No. 219. 4 feet 6 inches long, mounted complete, as shown on page 44 ... . $110 00

Any size or design made to order.

BUGGY.   PLOW.

Mounted complete.

No. 227. 42 in. long, mounted complete..$75.00   No. 228........ ....36 in. long..$24 00
     Any other size made to order.   " 228½...............54 "   .. 36 00

                                  Any other size made to order.

HORSE CAR.

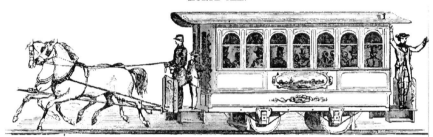

No. 220. 66 inches long, perfect model, with pair of " Ethans " attached, driver and
       conductor, mounted complete, as shown on page 50....................$200 00
                  Any other size made to order.

LOCOMOTIVE AND TENDER.

Mounted complete, as shown on page 50.

No. 221. 72 in. long, with Tender, perfect full-bodied model, extra work..........$200 00

" 222. 48 " " " " " " 150 00

" 223. Locomotive and Tender, 5 feet long............ .. .. 75 00

" 224. " without Tender............ .. .. 50 00

☞All our Vanes are made of copper, and gilded with finest gold leaf.

GRECIAN BANNERET, WITH SCROLL.

Banneret of Copper, Scroll Decorated in Gold and Colors.

No. 1. 3½ feet, 4 sided, as shown above, with scroll........................... $70 00
" 2. 3½ " mounted as shown on page 50, without scroll..................... 65 00
" 3. 4½ " 4 sided, as shown above, with scroll........................... 80 00
" 4. 4½ " mounted, as shown on page 50, without scroll................... 75 00

☞ All our Vanes are made of copper, and gilded with finest gold leaf.

TIFFANY VANE.

No. 276½. 5 feet long $45 00
"   277. 6   " 60 00
"   278. 7½ " 80 00

☞ All our Vanes are made of copper, and gilded with finest gold leaf.

CHURCH OR SCROLL VANE.

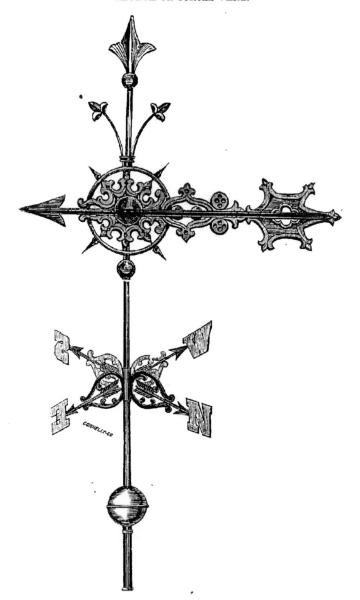

No. 282.	6 feet long	$90 00
" 283.	7 "	120 00
" 284.	8 "	140 00

☞ All our Vanes are made of copper, and gilded with finest gold leaf.

CENTENNIAL SCROLL VANE.—New Design.

No. 285. 5 feet long $89 00
  " 286. 6   " 100 00
  " 287. 7   " 130 00
  " 288. 8   " 150 00

☞ All our Vanes are made of copper, and gilded with finest gold leaf.

NEW DESIGN CHURCH VANE.

No. 313. 6 feet long $100 00
" 314. 7   " 130 00
" 315. 8   " 140 00

☞ All our Vanes are made of copper, and gilded with finest gold leaf.

NEW DESIGN SCHOOL AND LOCOMOTIVE VANE.

No. 6.   6 feet long $140 00
  "   6½ 7   " 155 00

NEW DESIGN BANNERET.

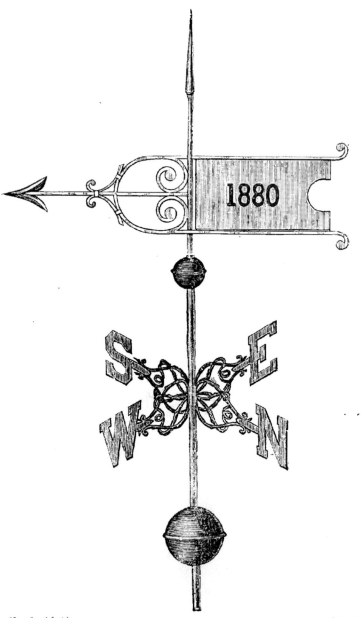

No. 18. 4 feet long $65 00
" 18½. 4 " 6 inches long.. 70 00

☞ Any number, monogram or initial cut in panel without extra charge.

SIGN VANE, WITH ANY NAME.

Letters in Name Decorated in Black.

No. 76½.	A.	6 feet long	$90 00
" 76½.	B.	7 "	120 00
" 76½.	C.	8 "	150 00

☞ All our Vanes are made of copper, and gilded with finest gold leaf.

METROPOLITAN SCROLL VANE.

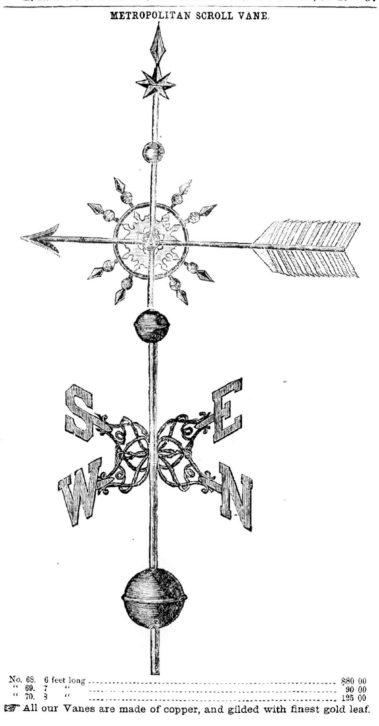

No. 68.   6 feet long $80 00
"   69.   7   " 90 00
"   70.   3   " 125 00

☞ All our Vanes are made of copper, and gilded with finest gold leaf.

BREWERS' AND MALSTERS' VANE.

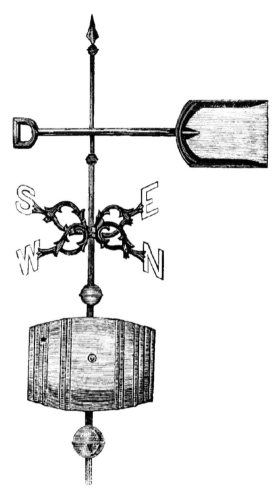

MALT SHOVEL AND BARREL, EITHER SEPARATE OR TOGETHER.

No. 52.	Shovel 5 feet long, Barrel raised 6 inches			$80 00
" 53.	" 5 "	without Barrel		60 00
" 53½.	" 6 "	Barrel raised 6 inches		95 00
" 54.	" 6 "	without Barrel		75 00
" 54½.	" 7 "	Barrel raised 7 inches		120 00
" 55.	" 7 "	without Barrel		90 00

☞ **Any** size Shovel made to order with **Barrel.**

SCROLL SIGN VANE WITH BARREL.—New Design.

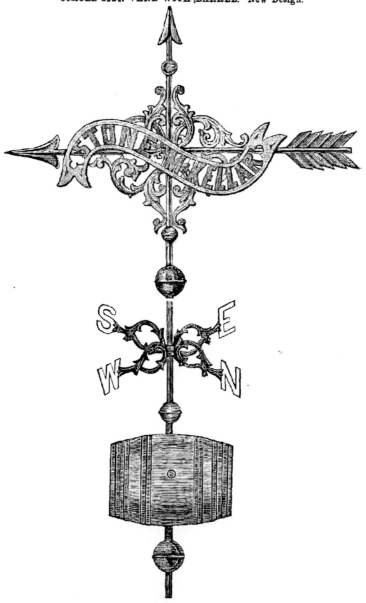

Made with any Name.

No. 63.	5 feet long, with Barrel raised 6 inches	$100 00
" 63. A. 6	" " "	125 00
" 63. B. 5	" without Barrel	80 00
" 63. C. 6	" "	100 00
" 63. D. 7	" 6 inches "	130 00

☞**Handsomely mounted with Spire, Letters and Balls complete.**

NEW DESIGN CHURCH OR SCROLL VANE.

No. 316.   5 feet long $75 00
"   317.   6   " 90 00
"   318.   7   " 120 00

☞All our Vanes are made of copper, and gilded with finest gold leaf.

ENGLISH BANNERET.

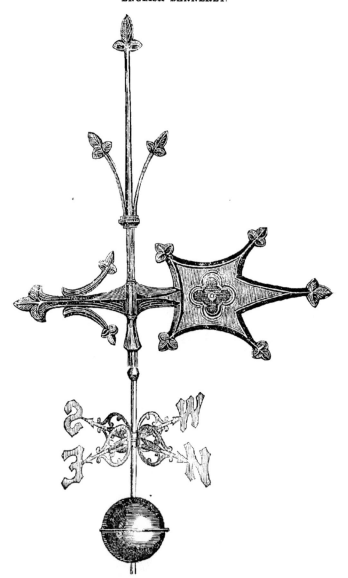

No. 2924. 3 feet 6 inches long...$50 00

☞ All our Vanes are made of copper, and gilded with finest gold leaf.

NEW DESIGN BANNERET, CROWN AND FINIAL VANE.

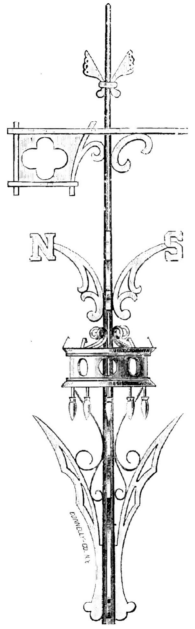

No. 319   Banneret, 4 feet long, complete as shown above........................$130 00

Gilded and decorated in any color. Any size made to order.

NEW DESIGN CROWN BANNERET.

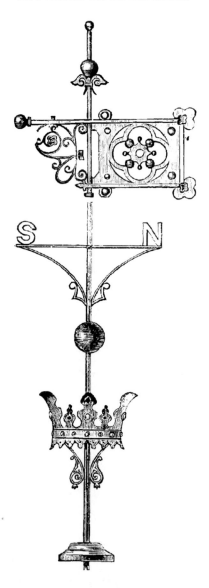

No. 13. Banneret 30 inches long, Crown 24 inches diameter........................$100 00

☞ All our Vanes are made of copper, and gilded with finest gold leaf.

CROWN BANNERET.—Copper and Galvanized Iron.

No. 301 A. Height from bottom of Rod, 9 feet 10 inches, 4 sides............ .....$125 00

☞ Banneret can be made with initial or ornamental device.

NEW DESIGN BANNERET AND SCROLL VANE.

No. 320.   Banneret, 3 feet long, scroll copper and gilded............................$100 00

"   321.   "   "   "   mounted complete, as shown on page 60............   50 00

DOMINICAN CROSS AND VANE.—New Design.

No. 302 A, 16 feet high, Copper and Brass, gilded...................................$350 00

☞ Any other design made to order.

ROMAN BANNERET.

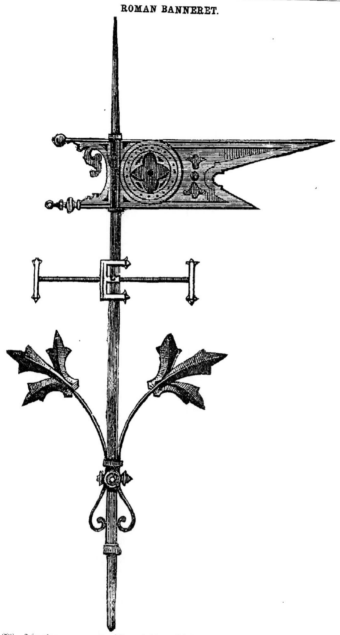

No. 290. 3 feet long, ornaments of Iron, 4 sides, gilded and decorated in any color. $70 00
"   291. 3 " 6 inches long, "   "   4 "   "   "   "   85. 00
"   292. 4 " long,   "   "   4 "   "   "   "   100 00

☞ **Vanes of any design made to order at reasonable prices.**

NEW DESIGN BANNERET AND FINIAL.

No. 322. 2 feet 9 inches long, as shown above.................................$44 00
" 323. 2 " 9   "   mounted, as shown on page 81...................... 50 00

☞ Banneret of copper and gilded, finial of iron, decorated in gold and colors.

NEW DESIGN BANNERET AND FINIAL.

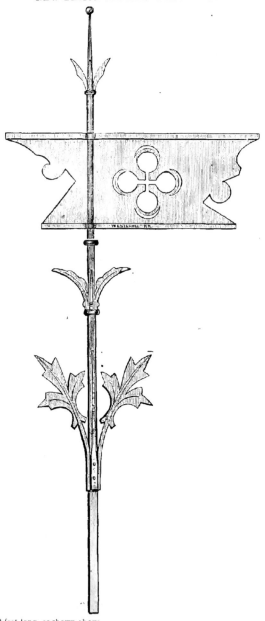

No. 324. 3 feet long, as shown above...$46 00
" 325. 3 " mounted, as shown on page 81.... .... 52 50

☞ Banneret of copper and gilded, finial of iron, decorated in gold and colors.

ANTIQUE INITIAL AND HORSE BANNERET VANE.

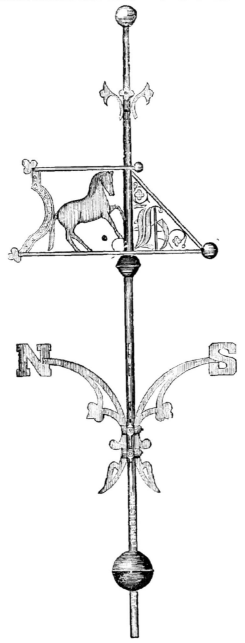

No. 5.   4 feet long, as shown above. $85.00
"   5½.   5   "   " 100.00

☞ Banneret of copper and gilded, points of compass of iron, decorated in gold and colors.

NEW DESIGN BANNERET.

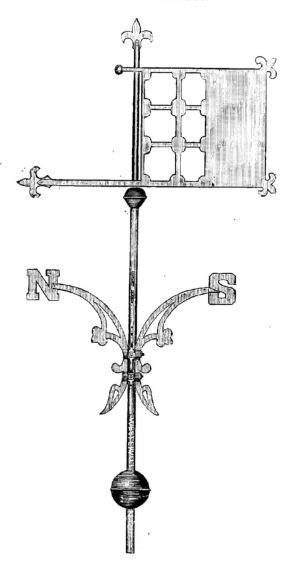

No. 326. 3 feet long, as shown above..$52 50

" 327. 3 " " on page 81... 47 50

☞ Banneret of Copper and gilded, points of compass of iron, and decorated in gold and colors.

NEW DESIGN BANNERET.

No. 328,   3 feet long, as shown above 350 00

"   329.   3   "   "   on page 81 .... 45 00

☞ Banneret of copper and gilded, points of compass of iron, and decorated in gold
and colors.

NEW DESIGN BANNERET.

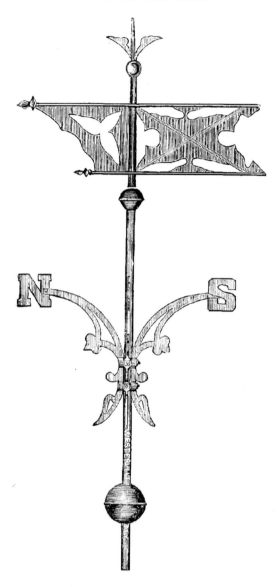

No. 330.   3 feet 6 inches long, as shown above $60 00

" 231.   3   "   "   "   "   on page 81 .... 55 00

☞ Banneret of Copper and gilded, points of compass of iron, and decorated in gold and colors.

NEW DESIGN BANNERET.

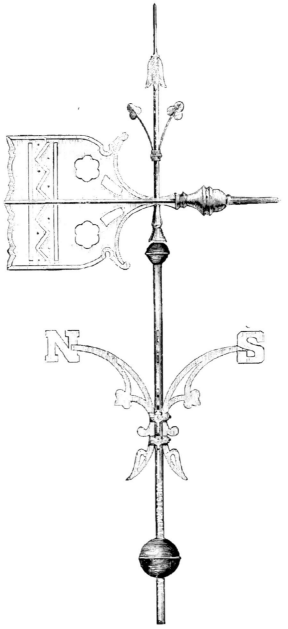

No. 332. 3 feet long, as shown above..$55 00
  " 333. 9   "   "   on page 81 .... 50 00

☞ **Banneret of Copper**, points of compass of iron, decorated in gold and colors.

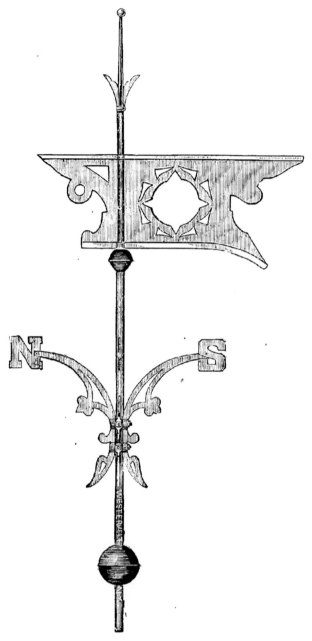

No. 334. 3 feet long, as shown above..$50 00
  " 335. 3   "   "   on page 81... 45 00

☞ Banneret of copper and gilded, points of compass of iron, and decorated in gold and colors.

NEW DESIGN BANNERET.

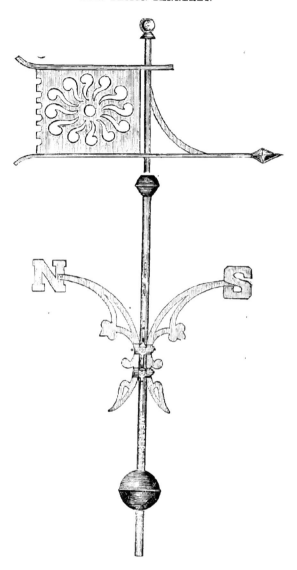

No. 336.   3 feet long, as shown above................................. .. ..$55 00

" 337.   3   "   "   on page 81........ .... 50 00

[☞ Banneret of copper, points of compass of iron, decorated in gold and colors.

NEW DESIGN BANNERET.

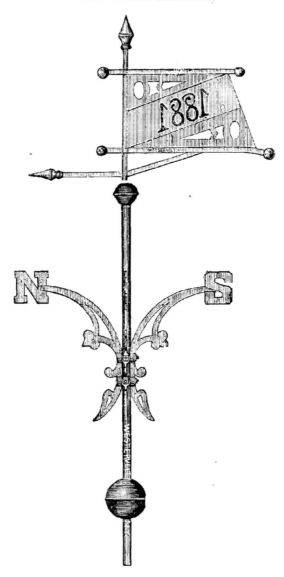

No. 338. 3 feet long, as shown above..$50 00

339. 3   "   "   on page 81..................................... 45 00

☞ Banneret of Copper and gilded, points of compass of iron, and decorated in gold and colors.

Any number or initial cut in panel without extra charge.

NEW DESIGN BANNERET.

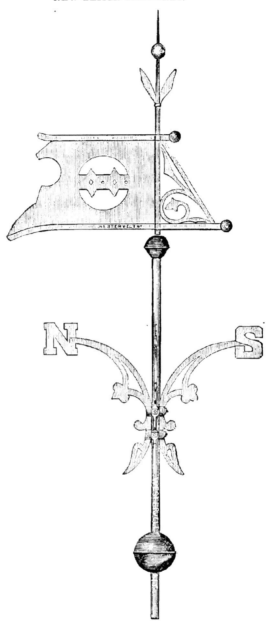

No. 340. 3 feet long, as shown above...$46 00

"   341. 3   "   "   on page 81...................................... .... 42 50

☞ Banneret of copper, points of compass of iron, decorated in gold and colors.

NEW DESIGN STAR AND CRESCENT BANNERET.

No. 342.   3 feet long, as shown above..$55 00
" 343.   3   "   "   on page 81...50 00

☞ Banneret of Copper and gilded, points of compass of iron, and decorated in gold and colors.

NEW DESIGN BANNERET.

No. 344. 3 feet long, as shown above..$55 00
"   345. 3   "   "   on page 81. .... 50 00

☞ **Banneret** of Copper and gilded, points of compass of iron, and decorated in gold and colors

NEW DESIGN BANNERET.

No. 346.   2 feet 6 inches long...$30 00

"   347.   3 feet long...42 50

☞All our Vanes are made of copper, and gilded with finest gold leaf.

ARROW VANE.

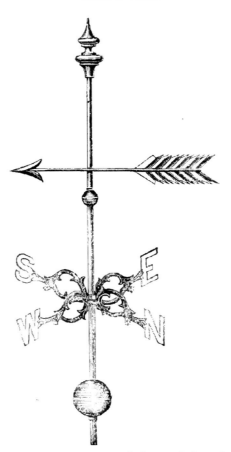

All our **ARROW VANES** are corrugated, thus greatly increasing their strength
and beauty.

No. 246 B. 96 inches long $100 00
"   246 A. 84   " 70 00
"   246   72   " 50 00
"   247   60   " 30 00
"   248   48   " 20 00
"   249   42   " 18 00
"   250   36   " 15 00
"   251   30   " 10 00
"   252   24   " 8 00
"   253   18   " 6 00
"   254   15   " 5 00
"   255   12   " 4 00

The above prices are with Spire, appropriate Letters and Balls complete.

CHURCH OR SCROLL VANE.

No. 256.	Scroll Vanes 12 feet long		$125 00		No. 265.	Small scroll, 4 feet long		$20 00
" 257.	"	10	"	100 00	" 266.	"	3½ "	18 00
" 258.	"	8	"	90 00	" 267.	"	3 "	15 00
" 259.	"	7	"	80 00	" 268.	"	2½ "	12 00
" 260.	"	6	"	65 00	" 269.	"	24 inches long	10 00
" 261.	"	5½	"	45 00	" 270.	"	18 "	8 00
" 262.	"	5	"	35 00	" 271.	"	15 "	6 00
" 263.	"	4½	"	25 00	" 272.	"	12 "	5 00
" 264.	"	4	"	23 00	" 273.	"	8 "	4 50

SCROLL VANE.

No. 22.   28 inches long, mounted complete, as shown above............................$14 00

LYRE BANNERET.—For Music Halls, &c.

No. 56.	2 feet 6 inches long	$20 00
" 57.	3 feet long	25 00
" 58.	4 "	35 00
" 59.	5 "	45 00

NEW DESIGN BANNERET.

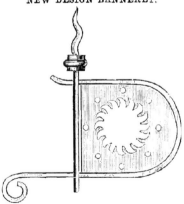

| No. 348. | 2 feet 6 inches long, mounted complete, as shown above | $30 00 |
| " 349. | 3 feet long, " " " " | 40 00 |

SCROLL HARP VANE.—New Design.

No. 350.   4 feet long.... ....$38 00 | No. 351.   5 feet............ ....$48 00

NEW DESIGN BANNERET.

No. 352.   2 feet long, mounted complete, as shown above.............. .... $2
  " 353.   3 feet 6 inches long, mounted complete, as shown above... .... 30 00

ROMAN SCROLL.—New Design.

No. 274.   3 feet long $20 00
"   275   4   "   .... · 25 00
"   276.   5   " 40 00

SPEAR HEAD SCROLL.

No. 279.   4 feet long, mounted complete, as shown above $20 00
"   280.   3½   "   "   "   "   " 18 00
"   281.   3   "   "   "   "   " 15 00

ROMAN SCROLL.—Old Design.

No. 237.	3 feet long.		20 00
" 238.	4 "		25 00
" 239.	5 "		40 00
" 240.	7 "		50 00

PEN VANE.

Especially designed and adapted for Newspapers, Libraries, Banks, Schools, Colleges, Academies, and other Public Institutions.

No. 241.	2 feet long, mounted complete, as shown above						12 00
" 242.	3 "	"	"	"	"		18 00
" 243.	4 "	"	"	"	"		25 00
" 244.	5 "	"	"	"	"		40 00
" 245.	6 "	"	"	"	"		55 00

SPARKLING VANE,

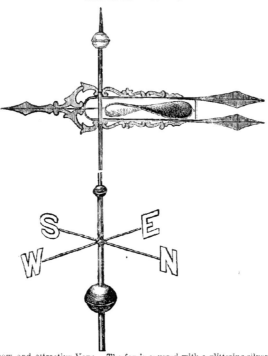

This is a new and attractive Vane. The fan is covered with a glittering silvery substance, making a very showy appearance while revolving in the wind.

No. 46.	4 feet long	$30 00
" 47.	5 "	40 00
" 48.	6 "	70 00
" 49.	7 "	80 00

FIREMAN'S CAP AND TRUMPET VANE.

No. 361. Hat 2 feet long, trumpet 2 feet 6 in. long, mounted complete, as shown above, $50 00
" 362. " 2 " 6 in." " 3 " 6 " " " " " 65 00

NEW DESIGN LYRE BANNERET.—For Music Halls, &c.

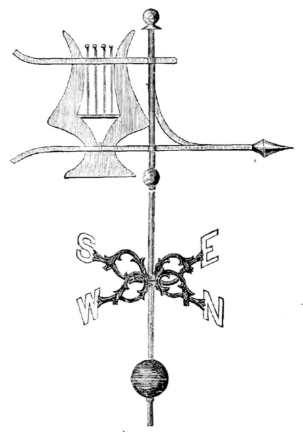

No. 354. 3 feet 6 inches long, double thickness.... .... $60 00

NEW DESIGN LYRE BANNERET.—For Music Halls, &c.

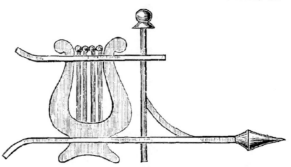

No. 355. 3 feet 6 inches long, single thickness, mounted complete, as shown above.. $40 00

☞All our Vanes are made of copper, and gilded with finest gold leaf.

INITIAL BANNERET.

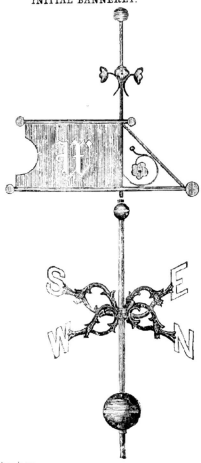

No. 22½	A.	2 feet 6 inches long	$30 00
" 22½	B.	3 " long	35 00
" 22½	C.	3 " 6 inches long	45 00
" 22½	D.	4 " long	50 00

Any initial, monogram, or number cut in panel without extra charge.

SCROLL WITH INDEX.

No. 73.	3 feet long, mounted complete, as shown above	$18 00
" 74.	3 " 6 inches long, mounted complete as shown above	22 00
" 75.	4 " long, mounted complete, as shown above	25 00
" 76.	5 " " " "	35 00

NEW DESIGN MONOGRAM BANNERET.

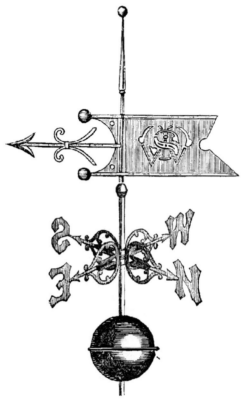

No. 14.   3 feet long $50 00
" 14½ 3 feet 6 inches long.. 58 00

Any number, monogram or initial cut in panel without extra charge.

NEW DESIGN INITIAL BANNERET.

No. 356.   2 feet 6 inches long, mounted complete, as shown above...................$30 00
" 357.   3 feet long,   "   "   "   " 40 00
" 358.   3 feet 6 inches long,   "   "   "   " 50 00

Any number, monogram or initial cut in panel without extra charge.

BANNERET, NEW DESIGN.

No. 7.   3 feet 6 inches long..$50 00
  "   7½. 4 feet long.....   .... 60 00
        Any number, monogram or initial cut in panel without extra charge.

SCROLL AND LOCOMOTIVE VANE.

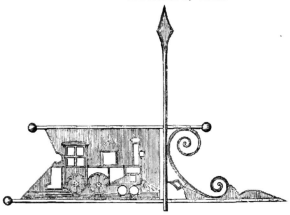

No. 8.   4 feet 6 inches long, mounted complete, as shown above....................$60 00
No. 8½. 5 feet long,   "   "   "   " 70 00

☞ All our Vanes are made of copper, and gilded with finest gold leaf.

NEW DESIGN INITIAL BANNERET.

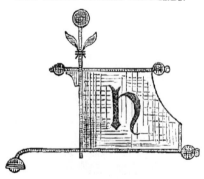

No. 11.   3 feet long............$45 00 | No. 11¼.   4 feet long............$60 00

Any number, monogram or initial cut in panel without extra charge.

NEW DESIGN INITIAL BANNERET.

No. 12.   3 feet long, mounted complete, as shown above..................................$40 00
No. 12¼. 3 feet 6 inches long, mounted complete, as shown above........................ 50 00

Any number, monogram or initial cut in panel without extra charge.

VANDERBILT BANNERET.—New Design.

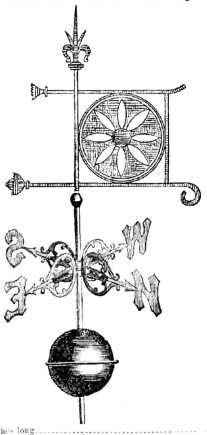

No. 16   2 feet 6 inches long...$40 00
" 16½   3 " long.. 45 00

Any other size made to order.

BANNERET.

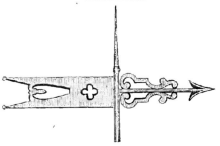

No. 62½. 2 feet long, mounted complete, as shown above.......................$18 00
 " 62.   3 "   "   "   "   "   " 20 00
 " 61.   3 feet 6 in. long, mounted complete, as shown above........ 25 00
 " 60.   4 " long, mounted complete, as shown above.................. 30 00
 " 59.   5 "   "   "   "   "   " 35 00

☞ All our Vanes are made of copper, and gilded with finest gold leaf.

BANNERET, NEW DESIGN.

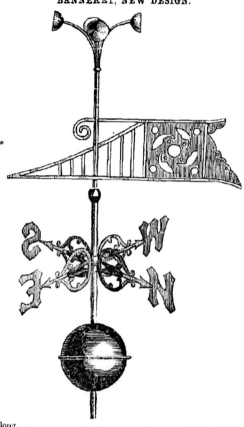

No. 9. 3 feet long $50 00
" 9½ 4 " 65 00

FRENCH SCROLL VANE.

No. 10. 3 feet long, mounted complete, as shown above $40 00
" 10½ 4 " " " " " " 45 00

Any size made to order.

NEW DESIGN BANNERET.

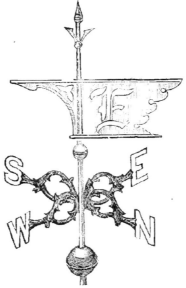

No. 15.   2 feet 6 inches long.. $35 00
" 15½ 3 "   long... 40 00

NEW DESIGN INITIAL BANNERET.

No. 259.   2 feet 6 inches long.. $30 00
" 360. 3 "   long... 40 00

NEWPORT BANNERET.—New Design.

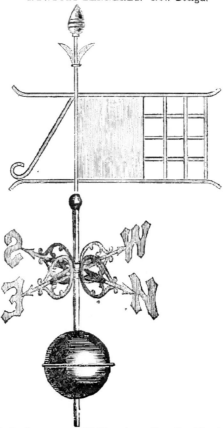

No. 17 2 feet 6 inches long.........$35 00 | No. 17½, 3 feet long........$40 00
Any other size made to order.

BANNERET.

No. 19 A. 3 feet long, mounted complete, as shown above.................. ....$35 00
" 19½ B. 2 " 6 inches long, mounted complete, as shown above..... .... 30 00·

MANHATTAN BEACH HOTEL BANNERET, BLUE AND GOLD.

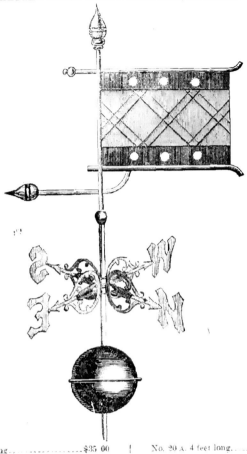

No. 20. 3 feet long................$35 00 | No. 20 A. 4 feet long...............$55 00

BANNERET.

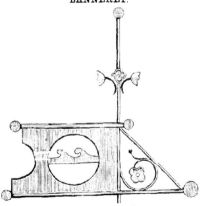

No. 20½ A. 3 feet long, mounted complete, as shown above $35 00
"   21 B. 2 " 6 inches long, mounted complete, as shown above.....................25 00

LIGHTNING CONDUCTORS.

GALVANIZED STAR ROD.

PLATINUM TIPPED POINT, GILDED.

TWIST COPPER WIRE ROD.

ALL SOLID COPPER BAND TWIST ROD, SHOWING COUPLING AND FASTENING.

COPPER-COVERED STAR ROD.

NEW YORK AGENCY FOR LIGHTNING RODS.

A. B. & W. T. WESTERVELT, 102 CHAMBERS STREET, N. Y.

NEW AND IMPROVED
NICKEL-PLATED, POLISHED BRONZE AND IRON
STABLE FIXTURES,

Newest Designs at Lowest Prices.   Send for Catalogue and Prices.

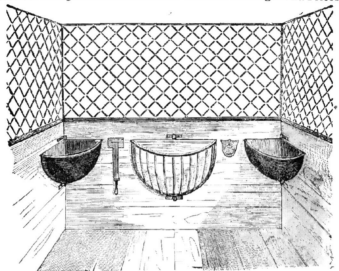

CAST CORNER MANGER.   **CAST CORNER HAY RACK.**

Corner Manger, Food Guard all around.

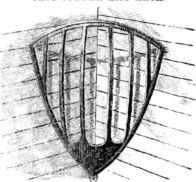

MANUFACTURED BY

A. B. & W. T. WESTERVELT,

No. 102 CHAMBERS STREET,

Cor. Church Street,   *NEW YORK.*

Estimates given for all kinds of Wrought and Cast-Iron Work, Copper
Weather Vanes, Finials, Crestings, &c.   Catalogues on Application.

G4552

CPSIA information can be obtained at www.ICGtesting.com
Printed in the USA
BVOW07s2147070514

352857BV00012B/592/P